To

Fast Sailings to Spain

SoftNet
Books

Fast Sailings to Spain

Tony Wailey was born in Liverpool in 1947

Fast Sailings to Spain

Tony Wailey

SoftNet
Books

First Published 2010 by SoftNet Books
SoftNet Books
P O Box 28582
LONDON N15 5WQ

ISBN: 978 0 9542731 3 2

Designed and typeset by iKraal
Printed in Croatia by Zrinski

For La Napolitana

"You made my life so rich
you know you could have been some money
and baby you're so sweet
you know you could have been some honey"

The Temptations
(Smokey Robinson, Motown 1964)

"Well sometimes I go out by myself
and I look across the water
and I think of all the things
that you're doing
and in my head I make a picture"

The Zutons
(Dave McCabe, Deltasonic 2006)

Contents

Part One

Part Two

Part Three

Acknowledgements

International Library of Poetry, *Cavan, Lady,
Blue* (2006), Liverpool Post and Echo, *Iron Man (1),
Athens, Amici Great Cities* (2007), Liverpool 800,
On the Edge La, Al Pujarra (2007), New York Review
of Books, *Maggie Cassidy* (2008), Nobel House,
Cavan (2008)

I am indebted to the University of the Arts, London
for a teaching fellowship which helped me complete
this book.

tw

Part One

Mozambique

I first came
when I was seventeen
by a poster of the Benfica Team
pasted to the wall
at the port of Lorenzo Marques.
She was serene
a wonderful woman
called Maria Chibalo
who handled me gently
did they feel the same?
Just a few years older
Mario Coluna, Eusebio,
Hilario de Conceio
playing their game
on the Lisbon river
dreaming of Africa,
Incala, Maputo?

Funny

I knew a girl once
she was funny
blonde hair and blue eyes
a real honey.
She married my mate
and came from Oregon
to ride on British Rail
after majoring at UCLA
in poetry
and ate a terrible pork pie
at Wigan
to say she'd done it
a la Phillip Larkin
with brilliant moonlit lines
crossing each other
under the moon
and a son to Dockery
but he didn't want the trouble
and she couldn't bear it.
She's back in America now
San Francisco, I think
and a practising Sufi
but I tell you
she was lovely.

Walton

The evening light
on the yellow block
paying off the debts
to society
I live between
five and eight
when they have TV
sometimes a 'phone
beyond the control
of the key
and I get wired
thinking of her
lilac as the night
reading Kerouac
from Fazackerley
where she lives
with the kids
and I get tired
and frightened
with love
from the inside
the walls, a life
the bars, a clock.

Aretha

When I was eighteen
a woman took a shine to me
it sometimes happens
one moment shaking tarpaulin
emptying bins
from that workhouse
called the sea
the next crossing the bridge
all washed down
cruising in a Mustang
across the town
the radio singing Aretha
New Orleans
below me
the bayou and the levee
Christ, and kissing
it raining buckets
and lightning
on the Mississippi.

Freshfield

The purple flowers
always with the hissing sound
of tides and rustled straw
behind the pines and lavender
perfuming the evening sea light
and river dreams.
In the summer of 1980
when I first met you
you brushed yellow drops
from white daisies
off your skirt
discarded lemonade bottles
of Vodka for the kids,
pushed them dripping by the trees
and made your way home.
Later you picked up the phone
and said "Do you want to come
round to ours?"

Author

The moon cradles the dock
perfuming the night
the smell of wood
of trees and bananas
Tony Lane writing
City of the Sea
by Cressington Park
on Spring evenings
overlooking Garston,
the departing tide
pools for the Mud Men.

Smithdown

Does the river still run through
the ribbons of your dreams
your great days
you said weren't there
evening sun from the water
raging at younger brothers
telling them where
they have to run
we raced towards the horses
careful of our laughter
then held each other
the sea whispering in the yard
the Carters laughing
the time we spent together.
You gave me the jib
said I was a slob
the look on my face
when you crossed the street
and said, "*C'mon love,
let's tie the knot,*"
the same sun
when I was young
still here
when our kids have gone
our house on Scholar Street
a pint in the *Mulliner*
on Smithdown road.

In Between

When Buddy came home
one sea green evening
booze in his hair
a yellow light of spring
dancing on his lips
the blonde wood yards
at Seaforth
steaming with his love
every bar singing
north of tobacco dock
the sun streaming
the stones ringing
the decks of
another ship
rose up to greet him.

Another Man

Who hasn't thought at night?
talking to ourselves
a few pints
about what we're doin'
and what we're going to do
I fucken told him
he's fucken had it
he won't do that again
I'll fucken have him
after all the rain, the sun
the lovely breeze
with a tune upon it
flowers suddenly looking up
standing or waving
orange and pinks
purples and yellow
white lilies
by the water
green by the river
waves comb in like butter,
one thousand nights
she whispered
I spent with him
could you love me
like he used to?

Lindenstrasse

The fine evening light
that comes with the tide
when the cloud breaks
and the sun shines
late in the afternoon
from the beach
or outside the bars
on Lime street.
I wrote a poem about it
once, it ended,
in America
I called your name
coming home
like an arriving freighter
cars fill up their lanes
by the Adelphi
outside the Yankee
the lighted pavement
is the colour of green.

Ad Absurdum

I couldn't see the point
I heard myself say
where was the goal?
the nets, the sun
where was the ball?
All there seemed
was a wooden cross
a crucifixion at Hall Road
and later
the largest Pickfords van
rolling down the road.
I think of them
when mist is on the river
when nights were long
as buttered toast
and the baby's yawning,
his little hands
we pressed together
these days strangely
trying to do what's best
it's that time
I love the most.

Misery

When you moan
I'm a miserable sod
I thank you God
for all the blessings
you bestow
you lift me up
when life is sad
you help me realize
what I do not know
a surly laugh
and smokers cough
you tickle my *Wellies*
from below
no religion
south of the belly
I taste your lips
of salted jelly
an Atlantic frozen
a wind lashed sea
your fierce laugh
comes to haunt me
off New York.

Naturalist

Nothing defines us like death
except knowing the places we're born
even tho' we've sworn never
to return, there is always a river
running through our souls.
I'd give my eye teeth
to see the sun again
over the water at Widnes
where the river bends like Brooklyn
under the green bridge.
The one Paul Simon looked over
in lovely weather
dreams we dreamed
hands we held together,
a sweet arse looks best
on a Scouse woman.

Coast

Late morning the sea mist
and a terrible sandwich
by dinner, rain on the lavender
then like love, a late sun
and afternoon laughter
the shallow surf on the strand
the yellow flowers behind the sand
himself bouncing on the bed
the pinewoods and the perfumed river
an evening sea house
brick and painted white
like picket fences in Connecticut
à la Anne Benson
a drink before his feeding
the house warming
his eyes closing and yawning
the books we read together
literature our mirror then.

Thebes

A liquid night ultramarine
the moon breaking free
storming into the city
from the Burbo Bank
can you remember
the dance of Thebes
we played on the beach
at Seaforth
after the Caradoc
or in town outside
The White House,
brimming with exigence
suffering desire
your eyes were the stuff
that destroyed pestilence.
By Hall Road station
you grabbed my hand
and guided me through trouble,
my banana gone
I held your face
against the moon
and wondered why I'd come
so soon.
And what I'd use
for returning fire
when you come raging
on the tide
do you see that sky
do you still dream?

Lady

By the lovely gardens
of Saint Phillip Neri
I saw Our Lady
cross Catherine Street,
in one hand she carried
fresh linen and *eau de cologne*
and in the other
the soul of my dead baby.
We think we know but we don't
the time in any season
when the spring tides set sail
from the bay of Buenos Aires
past Palermo, Sur and La Plata
sweet as blue September
wave caressing lonely wave
to cross the winter ocean.
Irregular as the night
they seep into her arms
her ravaged face
accepts their promise,
she smiles as she walks
towards Prince's boulevard
her face as luminous
as the moon
and casts her love
amongst the flowers.

Lover

All poets die intestate
one way or another
throwing rages at other sons
or their mothers
and then the lovers
all their troubles
their disappointment and frustrations
(with you)
avoid that at your peril
think of Ford Mustangs
New Orleans, Aretha Franklin
find a lawyer
dial that number.

North End

Bernard Fallon
the photographer
you know, the celebrity
who had an exhibition
at the Conservation Centre
on Whitechapel,
now he lives
in California
but still comes home
to see his family.
When I was a kid
with our auntie
in Crosby
his house had the only tree
a Horse Chestnut I think
outside
and his Old Man
a customs official
caught a bus home every evening
on a road that ran
through five thousand houses
and a thousand ships.
I remember him
walking placidly
in his raincoat
down our street
dandling the paper at his side
looking forward to his tea
towards the river
and the sea.

Iron Man (1)

Looking at the sea
I've forgotten what I've read
remembered what I'd forgotten
don't tell me what she said
if it was good or rotten
strings of seaweed, bottles and tar
bits of wood, nothing gets by me
sun on the water, in my head
died while I was alive
when you waved ta ra.
Your house beyond the dunes
flowers across the wall
it wasn't me who roared
"God is not afraid
there is a love inside."
You spread fire across my eyes
was it for the ride?
The radio playing tunes
anchors seize my feet
that's not me you see
dancing in the tide.

Other Lives

Having a beer
or reading a book
she's there
she's everything
inside me or
running with the sea
dancing in the tide
and from the Atlas Mountains
to the Cape
the great rivers unwind.
Running away with
the smell of wood
and taste of almonds
in her hair – my chair
on the veranda
only the darkness
and summer moon
protects me.
Tears wash my face
I'm telling you baby
you were a fool
to leave me.
Years later
I was going to tell
my third wife to fuck off
for infidelity,
I'm standing there
still by the chair
and thinking
hang on,
shouldn't it be me?

Part Two

Billy

All the Schools along that line
what are they learning
look at the coast, the docks?
Tell me son
what was that time?
Religion's hard to define
an opiate or only hope
son, that carriage was wired
a cathedral swinging on a rope
mobiles ringing
Windows Vista jingling
Ipods and Blackberrys
pinging or whirring
from besieged seats.
Billy sipped his whisky
awash in telephony
only soothed by drink
and company, he sang
"Waiting for the Sash"
and "The Old Rugged Cross"
but he didn't sing much
or say a lot
which was a blessing
his church was a why
his face was a mirror
a photograph
rather than a sphere
but with him always
a face here
and there a mystery

the back of a head
a fragment of a story
suddenly appears.
Kobe, Barcelona, Manila,
out of the picture
out of the cluster
try to muster
a ray of hope
go back to your son, son
help him with his *sats*
don't mess him up
no singing sea ports
no talking rivers.

Nana

Here we are again
sitting in the sun
watching the kids
play football
the horses run
smoking a cigarette
her first footfall
on a ferry
Beltast - Liverpool
to the final one
Winter, 1918 - 2007
and in the wind
the smell of rain
the same calendar
as Ingemar Bergman,
Patrick said "Nana
was a great gambler"
he's finding his feet
and I suddenly thought
this is the first summer
without her
then he said
fists full of shillings
"Gambling's - good"
and laughed
just like she used to
chasing numbers.

Stockwell Gardens

Smell from the Lime trees
after the rain
older Muslim fella
squashed cap
crumpled top
shirt sticking out
Fellahin
of Kerouac's Tangier
beat, worn out
looking for his supper
his smoke
his tea
his woman crying out
breathless
beneath the trees
their sweet smell
with his pain,
the same as
any other.

Climate Change

They laughed at us
down in Worcester
and played on Wednesday
because of the rain
Phil Taylor was sick
at the railway station
he knew what they'd say
back in the City
bad enough in '59
the year Lady died
it's flooding there now
fifty years later
but they're not laughing
like that again.

Don't Ask

Down these streets
you never saw a flower
just a pool of piss
in the corner
often with someone
lying in it.
The *for sale* boards
hanging down
gangs of *Scallies*
hanging around
someone on the phone
black, white or brown
they make no sound
taking that call
no colour bar here
a delivery made
just another day
but who the fuck
brings a kid up in this?

Original

When you're up singing
our boys are worth a million
remember the Nineteen Eighties
and the indigenous natives
being ceded the Black Hills
by the Reagan government
and receiving compensation
from the invading nation.
If the watery seven tenths
of the world is Ocean
the USA don't see it
between New York and Oregon
God and America
is not kind to the Indian
ask Tony Hillerman.
So stand up straight
and see your soul
in the dust and on the plains
it's them who take the bottle
it's them who pray
and fire the liquor
but who's to blame?
Think of Gordon Lightfoot
half Apache
writing *Early Morning Rain*
but he was Canadian
and went to Mass
every day.

Baudelaire

He'd always been the one
to scatter easy
the fruits of women
strange really with his teeth
but then he got pulled
by a real looker
a lilac orchid,
a child of the East
no siren this
enticing to rocks
off Gallo Lungo
the coast of Amalfi
his eternal soul
but with calm assurance
driving him forward
a damp flower
a burst of sunlight
on the banks of the Yangtze
the Yellow River
calling him home
a *poète maudit*
he'd always loved.

Nation

Liverpool is full of cunts
I should know
I'm one myself
but do you know
what makes me laugh
is when others think
they're good enough
who have no sense of
that bitter stuff
between chronic devotion
and intense disorder
or is it vice versa?
Their nationalism a sentinel
a state framework
born without resonance
but Liverpool
you'd be a poorer place
without every creed or race
and if it's the wind
that makes you spin
then make a hybrid
of us all.

Iron Man (2)

That Gormley scene
in Crosby
slate grey water
blue hills
waves blowing
across Wirral peninsula
rain and sudden light
rusted body
watching ships
wind on his face
sun on his head
stands dripping
spray spitting
around his nose
yellowed eyes
on Ireland, cries
"You've nailed me here
in the tide,
I've sung my song
I've played along
the tourists came
they dressed me up
it was all a stunt
I feel fucked up
now get me out
I've had enough."

Refuge

I heard her singing
by the Northern tube
she said she lived
on Hampstead Heath
but her gear was
from another scene
a flowered cardigan
Centre Point
or the West London
Mission. It said
stop all this
all the bollocks
all the niceness
rehab crack
give me back
my fucken demons.
She could have been
Johnny Caldwell
World Boxing Champion
lying flat
on Camberwell Green
his club the *Immaculata*
far from home.

Alchemy

Lying down by the river
under the sky
was it the Mersey or the Alt
or God that sent you
instead of the dogs
I usually get?
An angel
who blessed the flowers
and trees
and greeted me with kisses
in the chemicals and the piss
and brought a bottle with you
to fly between us.

De La Journeé

"Oh what a perfect day,
drink Sangria in the park."
Nick Cave played City Radio
woke up to pray in the dawn
strolled the city with coffee and pastry,
like James Joyce in summer Trieste
a couple of pints getting to know you
walk by the tide at Crosby
lunchtime pasta, wine - siesta
see the kids play football
bathe in the turquoise evening,
suggest Martini or Cinzano
dinner, promenade, deux expresso
make love to you like a lover
a trembled novena between the covers.
"Oh what a perfect day
forgot all about myself."

Killer

Half past eight
waiting at the bus station
cigarette hanging
people stretching
it makes them feel alive
I'm on the wrong side
there's no one here
to echo their smiles
sitting by the garage
Open the *Tennants*
a wee kingdom
as they say in Glasgow
a whole day to kill
a night time to wonder
wouldn't it be great
if she came back again
riding on a crate
she said she would
but I'm not betting
her horse will run.

Vera

A hot Spring day
in Liverpool
she got on the bus
humming a tune
she could have been
from Vera Cruz
the way she looked
and way she moved
she might die poor
she might live righteous
but shite!!!!
the way she looked
today
black and seventeen
and nobody's fool.

Miriam

I was poor here
and yellow and grey
in that poverty Camus spoke of
under the sun.
The rain, the browns and green
they were for other worlds
the Northern
with red and white suburbs
and taser guns.
Then you took me
to the Mersey
with the pink and lemon
flowers on the coast
and Billy's musical clubs
the Iona
the Linacre
the Taxi and Melrose
and I felt warm
amidst the laughter.

Virginia

Bathing lightly she emerges
furious and fragrant
"some pillow talk you have, cretin"
then,
"don't you want to come with us?"
she phones the kids
and quieter, the lover.
Donning silks and linens
we go to have our dinner
go to meet the others
writers at a Cretan convention
scrapping around for pieces
by Hieraklion
love songs of Kazantzakis.
"They're all cunts" she reaches
for more drink
at the hotel bar
and falls off her chair.
I help her up to bed
and wonder what I've said to
my wife of twenty five summers.

Shelter

When you venture out
on a cold afternoon
into the February air
and you're going
to see the Old Lady
who is all prepared
all you can really do
is say a prayer
Hail Mary full of grace
for the winter hospice
and give thanks for
the yellow light,
on her pink pyjamas
hiding the whirr
of the morphine driver
late sunlight
on the Hyacinths
their perfume fading
with her sweat
but no gloom here
the manner of her passing
a celebration
pray for us sinners now
my ex wife and child
live around the corner
I've felt better
but I feel all right
and I'll have a pint tonight
and praise the time
we spent together.

Our Ben

He was never obscure
nor particularly driven
but always pretty sure
of what he was doing
and he knew in his heart
he was just a part
of something bigger.

Intense locales or far horizons
none of us are certain
where we fit in.
There is always longing
always laughter
and sometimes losing
what we swim with.

Like his Grandad away at sea
or on the run, you let them in
when Scousers show up
as they always will
for food and drink or women
and he didn't want to be
different from that tradition.

When it came to lovers
he was never surer
the simple truth was
between each day and distance
he wanted to stay
with a basic theorem
love the woman who loved him.

Right Foot

Hard men, Carpenters?
retired now, still big hands
board the roaring bus
laughing
skilled men, respectable
pressed Terylene trousers
clean shirts
looked after, reposed
houses bought.
Protestants
signet rings peering,
from folded jackets,
hard nosed
going down the hill
for a drink,
remembering other worlds.
Never bring a communist
or a catholic to this door.

Ginny Smyth

She was born on
St Stephen's day
and died
on the Epiphany.
Twelve days after Christmas
taking down decorations
making her declarations
for the coming year.
A migrant from Ireland
that frenzied space
I can see her now
with her daughter
my Old Lady
and those five others
she adopted
from across the water.
An easy soul
She made our lives great.
Never one to make a fuss
she thought the world
of all of us.

Amici - Great Cities

Burning August Sundays
two European finals
twisted like fame
Kipling's "If"
or his pies and cakes
August Seventh 2005
August Fifth 2007
800 years since John
recognised the claim
the weather just the same
we left Liverpool
passed through Staffs
and onto Bucks.
Girls with horses
looked at us
in the raging heat
inland places
like Rome in the "80s"
the country arid again
red and yellow flowers
after the rain.
Two years ago we danced away
this Sunday at *Coopers*
before the train
now in ashes, the hurt,
frustration's hammer
from Athens the pain
that follows us
but even with the loss
the earth still wonders,

family and lovers
are sound
even the dog "Napoleon" laughs
it'll soon be Spring
and no doubt Riise
on Moscow and our banners.

Trapeze

At just this instant
I try to fix a place
by prayer
or meditation
or a fuck
if I'm in luck
so any room
hotel lounge
or whore slung
flophouse
becomes featured
what's best
is if it's taken
in sequence
like a medicine
in Church
on a chair
on a trapeze
off your head
on wine and beer
not looking down
measuring distance.

Club

Paddys at the tables
Blacks are at the bar
Sikhs playing pool
roaring at the Scots
some heinous crime,
a world banking crisis
I sit here chosen
frozen by injustice
drinking lager and wine
like Ignacio Silone
in the full madness,
a Scouser
made from every
mother's blood
a hybrid dancer
a chancer
the CSA don't bother me
my payments
are all on time
they hit the floor
like the Lehman Brothers
as regular as the bouncer.

Dancer

for Colin Jones

I photograph the others
I see what the punters don't see
the girls in tears
depression, disappointments, drudgery
it fascinated me.
When you see shots of Ballerinas
glamorous, perfectly posed
there is always another reality.
1963 was a big year for me
I married the dancer
Lyn Seymour.

Happy Birthday Ma

The Psychiatrist said
"Try to sever yourself
from extreme emotion.
it's not exactly the Soviet Union."
My ex wife hung her head
smiled, a fly in his web
and probably thought
"You don't need to be clever
to tell him that."
I felt their silent laughter
it always made me suffer
exonerated Stalin
a life between the covers
what was up with our Kevin?
The length of time I read?
What were we doing here?
What's wrong with loving
the dead?
Or venerating your mother?
What you shouldn't do I guess
is tell her all your troubles
or keep her in a jug
under the bed
a wad of roubles
tickling her enamel.

Des Philosophe

A cigarette outside the station
I wondered what they read
Jacques or Jean or Claude
then again whatever their *llamada*
Emile, Gilles or Roland
(that's Giles to you and me)
always ready to give us
the cut of their jib
what's the issue
where's the order
but are we that *trager* sad?
Being edgy carries a load
it gets you everywhere
or nowhere
but in between
there's a place
just like Alan Hansen's face
when he hears Bobby Joel
his American passion
or Derry Mathews fighting
at Liverpool Olympia
and Faron singing
with the Flamingoes
to you and me the old Locarno
on West Derby Road.
Come for a bevy Etienne
this is a Port City
sat beside the Ocean
with sea strewn inhabitants
prone to wonder, and
forest fires of the imagination.

Part Three

Opera

In Liverpool it's important
not to forget
where you come from
and not get
above yourself.
Passing the laundrette
I remember the Old Lady
boiling the washing
in a copper
that was new then
compared to the Bath
Houses on Beatrice street
they ran for my Nana.
Sitting in a bar in Napoli
I think of the Cisco Kid
and a bunch of scruffs
including me
in front of a TV
on the new estate
from the fifties.
Music from America
while I'm in Italy
but whatever your luck
don't pass the buck
I'll admit
I didn't love them all
back then
half of them were cunts
but when you're happy
with your stuff

it's a cheek to say
Hey Mate, look at me
at the Opera House
the San Carlo Metropolitani
look at me mate!!!
You'd soon hear them say
Who'd y'think you are
a fucken chocolate drop?
Better than us
better than your Ma and Da?

Uncle Pat

If there was another
you wouldn't know it
smell of salt
the river
seagulls calling
The Angelus at the
Blessed Sacrament.
For a Catholic
and a democrat
he'd never pay for a pint
outside the bookies
or Exhibition Centre
trousers flapping
hair flying
easy saying
always joking.
The great days
never there?
Better say prayers
for the future
but don't forget
this city was built
on Slaves and Sugar.

Marseilles

Sometimes with drugs
you don't know
when you've had enough
the same with drink
and sometimes women
you don't know
where it goes
just when you think
you've fired your stuff
another one comes up
and calls your bluff
I came by your district
the other day (by bus)
you're poor like me
it was the same
for all our family
but lover take care
you're from Naples
I'm from the 'Pool
don't think
you can break those rules
forget about mountains
and sunlit hills
I need *Sildenfil*
and crowded docks
a bevy to draw on
while watching the ships
a cigarette to smoke
after kissing your lips
a kindness I'm trying
to continue with.

Cavan

I stood under an awning
waiting for my son
not like Anthony Powell
and the one he'd "put" in School
then sat dreaming of Pliny
on a wall
listening to the rain.
I only shuddered at the thought
of the next arraignment
at what else he'd done.
Our Patrick again
a boy with the long gait
and twisted smile
and a look that sometimes
makes you want to run
hide behind the pain
wrap time within a ball
remember when he was young
that smile again.
I hope he finds his way
not deny him his terrain
like the son of Louis McNiece
in a back yard chopping wood
the axe falling again and again
despair at his father's stance
the sudden seed squandered
grandchild of an Ulster manse
the sunlight in the garden.
My son at his Nana's grave
when he bent his knee

and stood silent head down
still as a drum, an island sea
in the sunshine and the wind
his family all around
the love of his mother
that was my freedom.

Easy

She shopped at Primark
and worked in Netto
but when she saw him
she could never forget him.
She flew from John Lennon
down to Jerez
there's a convent there
next to the tourist office
with a square shaped cross
and his tortured body
nailed onto it.
His lovely face
wreathed by sadness,
by incense and the wine
she'd drink later.
She gave money to a vagrant
then bought a candle
and knelt to light it
for her daughter.
It's a fact
we're at our best
when we remember
generous acts.

Maggie Cassidy

Sometimes you hark back to
when a time was good
just natural really
to those years 1980 –1983
Friday football and coming home
sung masses on March evenings
going to the *Irish House* after tea
waking up Saturday
selling the *Morning Star*
back home for bacon and eggs
going upstairs for love and sex.
4.40 the football scores
a blanket around me
pulling on my kecs
4.55 the evening news
5pm *The Fonz* from American TV
scenes like the '50s Liverpool
then running to the Chelsea Bridge
passed the river
baked potatoes at supper
drinking wine the house full
laughter then going quiet
the kids gone out
25 years later I'm still on a train
with a Slovakian girl sat next to me
dressed in red white and green
but I remember that time
of migrants and love
when we were warm
and slumbered in Spring.

Bar

Rab or Phillip
Frankie or Seamus
you know them all
you let them in
to warm their fingers
around the fire
a thieves den
then you realise
going home,
beneath September trees
the crackle of leaves
you don't know them
not at all
in fact,
you know fuck all
it's just gassing
but you're not alone.
"I'm going to Prague tonite
to follow the Arsenal."
"Is that right Frankie?"
"Fucken right, tonight."
The flame is ours
to give or burn.

Waterfront

Will we ever make history
in circumstances of our own
choosing?
Awash in telephony
calling upon lovers I'd known
asleep in their mystery
their snores a polselmy
like rhythms of the sea.
My greatest days
I don't care
make no sense to me
without a prayer.

Athens

There's a word you don't want
used in Liverpool
"Surge" is the term
like Gainsburg once sang
or Alan once decreed
when he arrived in 1965
or Leone visualised
Once Upon a Time
in America
when Seymour Street
made our suits.
It reared its head in Athens
ancient as the eye of Sophocles
"Lucky everyone still in one piece"
texts Terry O'Neill.
Christened by the river
a tide that runs within us
we don't speak of it here
nor let others hurl against us
but let the Blessed
rest in peace
and resist its urge
to hurt or seduce us,
never let us walk alone
or suffer that darkness.

Between Rivers

Mary the Catholic Queen
would not let saliva
be applied
into the baptised mouth
of her son James.
A spit in the gob
common for left footers
and Scots at that time
while I stood by
a lamp, a tree
a bridge,
in the rain
waiting by the tracks (for a train)
on a Sunday afternoon
near Stirling
fucking miserable
thinking of Alexander Trocchi
and his leather jacket
and Jock Stein's mate
who ran the Italian café
with his daughters
and mourned each day
after 1985.
I was leaving for Glasgow
sometime later
but I was singing
Yeh yeh yeh.

Mezcla

Pennines under snow
geese across low sky
my shadow appears
over shoulder
sloping
between star grass
and Marshside
ice and blue morning
the colours of the Argentine
St Stephen's day
like one of Gogol's army
I march to the coming year
with an epitaph

He took it on
he offered them out
he brought it down la'

Hemingway talked
about the earth moving
'For whom the bell tolls'

The earth turning, Ingrid Bergman
saw the hills, the joins and bumps
of love, the only solution

'be humble
be always humble'
said Miguel de Unamuno.

Call Her

Who hasn't thought
at night
talking to ourselves
a few pints
without the burden
about what we're doin'
what we're going to do
then the woman
I saw her last night
in the café.
She looked good
she took me
around the corner
and gave me a blow job.
Please blessed lord
take us forward
let us know
where we're going
because I don't know,
am I lucky
or just troubled?
If desire is nothing
but a spasm, a jangle
why do I fight so hard
to stay with you?

Before the Fire

The most beautiful September
I can remember
right from the start
it turned me on,
pints of *Kronenbourg*
in sourball colours
of the Indian summer,
Liverpool on the cusp
the sun in the bar
the women looking good
the hot city streets
dusty and tender.
Madonna de la Rosa
crawling to Pompei
from Naples on her knees
grateful to be born
in the oranges
and the dust.
It's not easy
sometimes to reason
torn from violence
promising love
what did we think
we were thinking of
a holy lady
a third interregnum
a golden certitude?

Anda

Bigote's bar restaurant
Sanlucar de Barrameda
like one of Hemingway's
Pamplona novels
except seventy years later
all down from *Feria*
Jerez de la Frontera
just like "*Fiesta*"
4 o'clock doctors
and fat men gulp Tapas,
white faced dineros
dark glasses, down Fino
the tiled floor heaving
unwashed chancers
every corner shouting
at barman white shirted
mas vino, tapitos
sun on the water
fish and mariscos
ship back to Bonanza
the port of the river
Columbus's third venture
men who had never
made beds, washed dishes
but know about horses
know about dancers
smoke at the entrance.

Celebration

Would he urge you
when you're ripe
like a tree
for praying
to let you know
you're not just a wipe
across the windscreen
a bleep
in the credit card system
a piece of tripe
offal from his guts
would he show you
the beauty of Aquinas
free will and conscience
consoled by love
and Mary the Virgin?

On the Edge La'

I was just eighteen
when I first went to Seville
up the river
if you know what I mean
you learnt a thing or two
there about women
dancing and singing
clacking hands on wooden things
it made you feel good
any Scouser would
especially with a bit of grub
but fifty years older
the evening's colder
I just take *Prostease*
and a few smooth Tetley's
sitting in the Taxi club.
Someone once said
Liverpool's full of piss heads
but he was of a bitter hue
and couldn't stand silver boots
like we wear in here
dancing the Guadalquivir.

Warming

Sat in a lemon light
I knew everything would be
all right.
In the garden
my lover slumbers alongside me
my son gone back to his mother
the yellow days
soothe a global warning
salt fires the earth
I don't care, I'm enjoying
crickets maddened by the dusk
birds thrumming, wasps buzzing
her strange dance and drumming
in the wooden lilac,
I'm just fine
here on my bench
even if the day is coming
drinking *Jack Daniels* and lager
forget the dreaded funerals,
her lovely fullness
fires the colours
of an Indian summer.

Al Pujarra

My wife is in trauma
but I'm in Granada
eating caracoles.
The kid is on crack
I've just got the sack
but in Granada
there's great guacamole.
The other one's wasting
hasn't eaten for ages
says she's dyslexic
can't read the packet
but by the Alhambra
the chicken's fantastic.
My lover is worried
about her mother
but I don't see
that's to do with me
and this flan of el moro
is really sweet.
Here in Granada
I haven't a euro
with a wind you can't fight
and a hill for the night
- it nearly did for Laurie Lee -
when the Jefe' finds out
this Scouser will swing.
So give them a canto
and order a tazo
they can't kill a dancer
I'm drinking Lepanto
I'm smoking a puro.

Red

We test the firmament
towards the burning West
the sky looks down in wonder
at how we spend the time
in a bubble by the cube,
a theorem of tall design
or a sailing, that's the trouble,
without women
a ball that makes us run
and separates us all
do we know
if there's plenty
more to come
or none at all
do we know we're fucked
or when we're at our best?

Yellow

Do you sometimes wonder
rubbing stones beneath the sun
trying to get a blaze
going
just what we've done.
There ain't no home
for truth beauty justice
without the sower
always there / even in despair
otherwise a homelessness
that makes us nomads,
no matter what we sing
different stars bring us home
and let us know we're free
we do not always live alone
in the yellow light of Spring.
Will it ever be understood
through the pain
and through the blood
if you'll ever give us time
to know, or spend a life
learning to live?

Blue

I think of you when
blue is in the trees
when orange fires the dusk
your tattered sheepskin and white roll top
clinging to your jeans
your stolen boots from Hugo Boss
you said, *"I'm aching for a baby"*
and raised your eyes to the Irish Sea
your dice flung laughter without the fury
at all I love the most.

Film 68

Pulling down a young woman's
knickers
after she's twiddled herself
stupid
is a wonderful experience.
Antonioni used to say
the scent of a woman
is heaven for any man.
Absent
love has a feature
a certain figure
like luck or a number,
when you're gone
that's the time
for others to wonder.
Eating my scran
I'd say
that's between
me and Jesus.

Cab

Driving these things
when I was flush in 1980
working five and a half days
seeing me Tart
going to eat
then onto the parties
Ian Rush was on
350 quid a week
and I'd double that
not any more
we've got three girls
but we had a ball
they still call us
the ears of the city.

Church

She glides between
the sun and showers
up by my old lady's church
raindrops on the flowers
how beautiful is love
that shines down upon us.
By the mouth of the river,
Freshfield lavender
patches of green and brown
Buddleia and straw
rustle by the railway lines
in the lee of her smile.
Pink lupins
yellow dandelions
white nosegays
seem just fine
shaking and blowing
along the tracks.
Her party eyes
dance like fireflies
blaze like a Satyr's
on this Sunday in Summer.

Two Augusts

Here is the Alt before the tide
it really does leap here
by the broken jetty
the Cormorants we saw
last winter
you can hear the guns
from Altcar
and there in the distance
its changing course
stagnant by the prison
where Smigger was murdered
and poor Rhys
killed in his football kit
was just an innocent.

Basco

Bilbao without Franco
a bright sparkle of light
across the Nervion
rain and bridges
the ships went under
by the Casco Viejo
sometimes in sun
but always the Chubasco
photos of Potato Jones
making his run
with food and guns in '36
and Stalin in his corner
crowds lining the river.
Boats all gone now
but by luck we've come
to satellite cafés
and white hotels
muscling their turn
at the water
and lovely girls laughing
with old men
by the Guggenheim Museum
all light and angles
a maritime cathedral.

Iron Man (3)

A sea rose plucked
from the river Alt
a warm upstairs
kids and dogs
that's what I want
a house and a wife
who bellows *Basta*
and serves the pasta
with love and tomatoes.
I saw her rose today
with a special look
and my scales softened
like the petals
and were blown away,
I watch the way
the river bends,
tired of running
I don't want to catch up
I tell you la'
beneath the sun
for a man of iron
I think I've pulled.

Sonnet

I've been lucky
sometimes it rained women
but with friends now
on this winter anniversary
by Hall Road beach
Waterloo and Crosby
a lover of thirty summers
beside me and the Gormley's
I feel blessed
especially by Lydia Street
and the dockers umbrella.
A few bevvies, a blow through
in good cheer at the local bar
The Marine on South Road
she leans over
and I go to the toilet
an easier flow
like tears unfolding
a constant stream, yippee
no *Prostease* this Christmas
between us we've got six kids
but I needed that kiss.
bring on the New Year.

Champagne

She was such a generous spirit
she brought me *Bollinger* on Christmas Day
she hasn't got a pot to piss in
we lie in bed drinking and laughing
it pours down my face like a Christening.

Port

When all the kids
are looked after
when all the loving
is done
when every part of perfection
has been drained
from the perfect sun
please leave us the sea
and the moon
and your blessed mother,
a horizon to pray upon
like an altar
snort cocaine at sixty three
and dance again.

Mid January

I came last night
like a midnight train
with a woman from Naples
who talked of a writer
called Elana Ferrante
and kissed me quietly
for St Anthony's day.